P9-DNP-892

CURRENT SCIENCE®

CREEPS
of the Deep

Explore the Ocean's Strangest Creatures

By Charles Piddock

Reading Adviser: Cecilia Minden-Cupp, Ph.D., Literacy Consultant
Science Curriculum Content Consultant: Debra Voege, M.A.

Gareth Stevens
Publishing

Please visit our web site at **www.garethstevens.com.**
For a free color catalog describing Gareth Stevens Publishing's list of
high-quality books, call 1-800-542-2595 (USA) or 1-800-387-3178 (Canada).
Gareth Stevens Publishing's fax: 1-877-542-2596

Library of Congress Cataloging-in-Publication Data

Piddock, Charles.
      Creeps of the deep : explore the ocean's strangest creatures / by Charles Piddock.
         p. cm. — (Current science)
      Includes bibliographical references and index.
      ISBN-10: 1-4339-2059-X   ISBN-13: 978-1-4339-2059-2 (lib. bdg.)
      1. Deep-sea animals—Juvenile literature. I. Title.
      QH91.16.P53   2010
      591.77—dc22   2009006800

This edition first published in 2010 by
Gareth Stevens Publishing
A Weekly Reader® Company
1 Reader's Digest Road
Pleasantville, NY 10570-7000 USA

Copyright © 2010 by Gareth Stevens, Inc.

Current Science™ is a trademark of Weekly Reader Corporation. Used under license.

Gareth Stevens Executive Managing Editor: Lisa M. Herrington
Gareth Stevens Senior Editor: Barbara Bakowski
Gareth Stevens Cover Designer: Keith Plechaty

Created by **Q2AMedia**
Editor: Jessica Cohn
Art Director: Rahul Dhiman
Designer: Tarang Saggar
Photo Researcher: Kamal Kumar
Illustrators: Indranil Ganguly, Rohit Sharma

Photo credits (t = top; b = bottom; c = center; l = left; r = right):
David Shale: cover, Emin Kuliyev/Shutterstock: title page, Bob Eggleton: 5, Shutterstock: 6, Chuck
Babbitt/Istockphoto: 7t, Specta/Shutterstock: 7b, Reniw Imagery/Shutterstock: 10, Mircea Bezergheanu/
Shutterstock: 11, Vakhrushev Pavel/Shutterstock: 12, Frantisekhojdysz/Shutterstock: 13, Ian Scott/
Shutterstock: 14, Carl-Werner Schmidt-Luchs/Photolibrary: 15t, Istockphoto: 15b, Karen Gowlett-
Holmes/Photolibrary: 16, Dr. J. Metzner/Photolibrary: 17, Dreamstime: 18, Kelvin Aitken/Photolibrary: 19t,
Dreamstime: 19b, OAR/National Undersea Research Program (NURP)-Univ. of Connecticut: 20, Omkar.A.V/
Shutterstock: 21(background), Woods Hole Oceanographic Institution/National Science Foundation:
21, Andre Seale/Photolibrary: 22, Deepseaphotography.com: 23, Franco Banfi/Photolibrary: 24, Kim
Reisenbichler © 1996 MBARI: 26, David Fleetham/Getty Images: 27, Solvin Zankl/Naturepl: 28t, David
Shale/Nature Picture Library (inset): 28c, Norbert Wu/Photolibrary: 29, NOAA Photo Library: 30, Joze
Maucec/Shutterstock: 31t, E. Endo/U.S. Geological Survey: 31c, Pichugin Dmitry/Shutterstock: 31b, NOAA
Photo Library: 32t, Frans Lanting/Corbis: 32b, Dr. James P. McVey/NOAA Photo Library: 33t, Mary Evans
Picture Library/Photolibrary: 33b, Bob Cranston/Photolibrary: 34-35, Dr. Bob Embley/NOAA Photo Library:
36 and 37t, National Deep Submergence Facility/WHOI: 37b, A. FILIS/Associated Press: 38b, Istockphoto:
40, NOAA/Monterey Bay Aquarium Research Institute: 42, LynnSeeden/Istockphoto: 42-43, Shirley
Pomponi: 44, Ian Scott/Shutterstock: 47
Q2AMedia Art Bank: 6, 8-9, 11, 17, 23, 25, 35b, 38t, 39, 41, 43

All rights reserved. No part of this book may be reproduced, stored in a retrieval system,
or transmitted in any form or by any means, electronic, mechanical, photocopying, recording,
or otherwise, without the prior written permission of the copyright holder. For permission,
contact **permissions@gspub.com.**

Printed in the United States of America

1 2 3 4 5 6 7 8 9 12 11 10 09

CONTENTS

Words in **boldface** type are defined in the glossary.

Chapter 1

In Search of Sea MONSTERS

An artist's illustration of a giant squid

Two scientists sat on a boat, watching an underwater camera. A line with bait was nearly 3,000 feet (914 meters) deep in the ocean. Suddenly, there was action! A huge creature was on the line, fighting to free itself.

CAUGHT IN ACTION

One of the creature's **tentacles** tore off. The wounded animal escaped into the dark depths. Yet the camera had captured the animal forever. The first pictures of a live giant squid were finally on film.

The sighting took place in 2004 about 800 miles (1,287 kilometers) south of Japan. For hundreds of years before then, giant squid had washed up dead on the shores. People told stories about battles between big squid and whales. At last, the giant creature was on video. The animal was not a monster. Instead, it was a wondrous being adapted to living and feeding at great depths.

Not so long ago, people imagined that the sea was full of strange creatures. Humans feared that giant snakes and lizards lived in the depths. Progress in science has calmed those fears, however. **Oceanography** is the study of the ocean. **Marine biology** is the study of sea life. Oceanographers and marine biologists have helped us better understand life in the sea.

Attack of the Kraken

The kraken is a huge sea monster from legends. This creature was said to live in the ocean near Norway and Iceland. People who claimed to see the kraken described it as a giant octopus. One story described a beast "the size of a floating island."

In 1752, Erik Pontoppidan wrote *The Natural History of Norway*. He said the kraken could pull a warship to the bottom of the ocean. Another observer claimed the creature surfaced and started "spurting water from his dreadful nostrils and making ring waves around him, which can reach for many miles."

The legends were probably tall tales about giant squid. No one has claimed to see the kraken in modern times.

The kraken starred in scary stories.

ALL WET

Water covers more than 70 percent of Earth's surface. The surface waters have waves, which pack plenty of power. Yet the active surface is only the tiny top layer. The surface represents less than 1 percent of the ocean's 336 million cubic miles (1.4 billion cubic km).

On average, the ocean is 2.3 miles (3.7 km) deep. Different kinds of life live in different layers of the water. This sea life ranges from tiny one-celled plants to the giant blue whale. About 85 percent of plant life on Earth is made up of the single-celled plants in the ocean.

FAST FACT

The ocean holds 99 percent of the "living space" on Earth.

WATER WORLD

Earth has five main oceans.

ARCTIC OCEAN

ATLANTIC OCEAN

PACIFIC OCEAN

INDIAN OCEAN

EQUATOR

SOUTHERN OCEAN

LIVING WATERS

Every day, scientists learn more about unusual sea creatures. Long ago, people thought whales were sea monsters. Later, researchers learned more about whales and their habits, which calmed people's fears about the animals.

When *Jaws* hit theaters in 1975, the movie fueled people's fear of sharks. After the film came out, many beachgoers stayed away from the water. Then scientists helped people understand the way sharks act. Now many people know that few sharks attack humans. More people realize that sharks are an important part of the balance of life in the sea.

This book is a voyage into the depths to observe fascinating marine animals. What kind of world has shaped these amazing creatures?

Science of the Sea

Marine biologists study sea life. They usually specialize in one area. Physical oceanographers study the sea's physical properties— for example, temperatures, **currents**, and waves. Chemical oceanographers study the water's chemicals. Geological oceanographers examine rocks and minerals in the sea.

Climate research is an important area of oceanography. The ocean alters climate. The water's temperature affects what happens in the air and on land. A warmer ocean could increase the number of hurricanes. A slight change in currents could mean a harsh winter. Climate change can also affect animals and plants that live in the ocean.

How do researchers collect information? Sometimes, they get help from **satellites** and robots. Ocean research has revealed many of the sea's secrets, but much is left to discover. In some ways, scientists know less about the ocean than they do about the far-off planet Mars!

The ocean floor is a new frontier for explorers.

IN THE ZONE

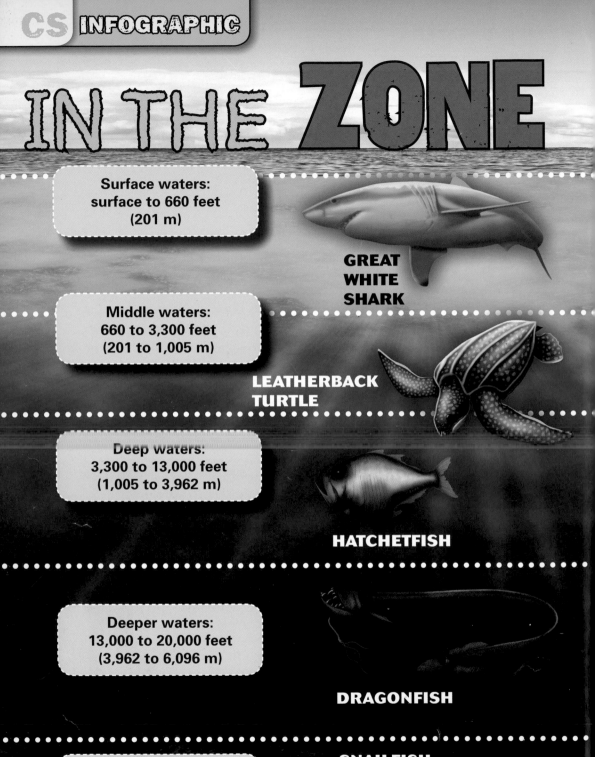

Surface waters:
surface to 660 feet
(201 m)

**GREAT
WHITE
SHARK**

Middle waters:
660 to 3,300 feet
(201 to 1,005 m)

**LEATHERBACK
TURTLE**

Deep waters:
3,300 to 13,000 feet
(1,005 to 3,962 m)

HATCHETFISH

Deeper waters:
13,000 to 20,000 feet
(3,962 to 6,096 m)

DRAGONFISH

SNAILFISH

Deepest waters:
20,000 to 36,200 feet
(6,096 to 11,034 m)

Oceanographers usually divide the ocean into five zones. The depth of each zone determines how much light reaches it. The depth also determines what kinds of creatures can live there.

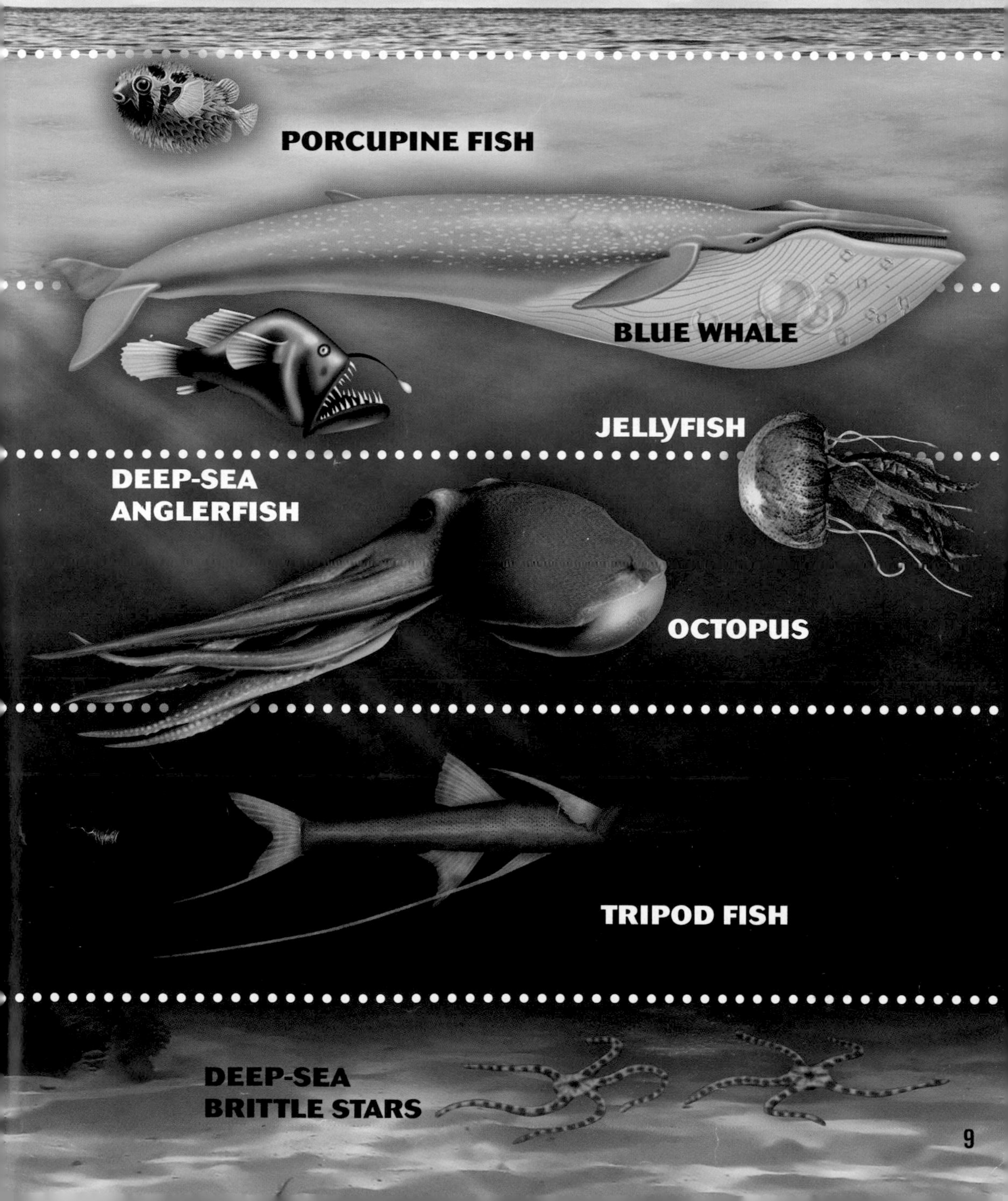

PORCUPINE FISH

BLUE WHALE

JELLYFISH

DEEP-SEA ANGLERFISH

OCTOPUS

TRIPOD FISH

DEEP-SEA BRITTLE STARS

Chapter 2

THE SUNLIT Sea

Surface waters: From the surface to 660 feet (201 m)

The sunlit sea is the part of the ocean that most people know best. Here, people swim, sail, and surf. This zone is also the feeding ground for millions of seabirds, dolphins, and other sea life.

IN THE NEIGHBORHOOD

Sunlight warms the surface waters. Many of the strange creatures that live at great depths spend their infant stage at the surface. The babies swim in the sunlit waters as they grow.

Tiny plant and animal organisms called **plankton** grow rapidly in this zone. Plankton provide food for fish and other creatures.

Where there are plenty of fish, there are plenty of **predators** ready to eat the fish. Surface waters are home to animals that can be dangerous to humans, too. Many sharks feed in this zone. Big rays, such as the manta ray, spend time in the surface zone. So do stinging creatures, such as the Portuguese man-of-war.

Strange but True

What makes a jellyfish a jellyfish? The creature does not have a brain, lungs, or gills. Jellyfish are 95 percent water. They take in oxygen through their thin skin. To swim, jellyfish shoot out jets of water. These creatures never stop growing. They may look harmless, but stay away from them! Jellyfish have a painful sting!

One especially strange jellyfish, the box jellyfish, has 24 eyes. The creature can see all around itself, but the picture is blurry.

Different kinds of jellyfish live in waters from the surface to the deep sea.

UNDER PRESSURE

At 300 feet (91 m), you are halfway through the surface zone. The water is still and calm. Even hurricane-force winds running over the water do not reach this level. If you were swimming here, you would not feel calm, however. You would feel as though you were being crushed.

The ocean is a powerful force of nature.

Have you ever jumped into a pool? If so, you have felt the weight of water. At the bottom of a deep pool, you feel pressure in your ears. As you go deeper in the ocean, pressure builds. That pressure is the weight of the water above as it presses down. Scientists measure pressure in units called **atmospheres**. The pressure at **sea level** is 1 atmosphere. For every 33 feet (10 m) you descend in the ocean, the pressure increases by 1 atmosphere. Divers need special equipment and training to stay safe.

OCEAN SNOW

At the bottom of the surface zone, there is "ocean snow." Using a camera and a powerful light, divers can see white particles floating and drifting. The particles are not like snow on a mountain. The bits are waste products from the life above. They include dead plant and animal parts. Everything that has not been swallowed by something drifts down. The ocean snow drops to lower levels of the sea. There, the snow provides other creatures with a meal.

To go below the surface, divers need special equipment, such as a wet suit, fins, an air tank, and a mask.

WHAT DO YOU THINK?

What might happen if "ocean snow" disappeared?

CREATURES OF THE SURFACE ZONE

The hammerhead shark is among the unusual surface creatures. These sharks use their oddly shaped heads to pin down **prey**. Hammerheads can grow as long as 20 feet (6 m). They can weigh up to 1,000 pounds (454 kilograms). Hammerheads eat other sharks and fish. Stingrays are their favorite food.

Stingrays move through this zone by flapping winglike growths on their sides. Some species are as small as the palm of your hand. Others are 14 feet (4 m) wide and weigh more than 3,000 pounds (1,361 kg). These fish have a sharp stinger on the tail. The stinger gives off poison.

The Portuguese man-of-war lives in this zone, too. This creature is actually a colony of four animals attached to one another! The animals float above water using an "air bladder" as a sail. These creatures have poisonous tentacles as long as 65 feet (20 m). The Portuguese man-of-war has a powerful sting. It can cause severe pain to humans. A sting can even be deadly.

FAST FACT
With an eye on each side of its wide head, the hammerhead can see all around itself.

The hammerhead shark lives in warm waters of the Atlantic, Pacific, and Indian oceans.

14

A bull ray like this one killed TV star Steve Irwin.

Danger Down Under

Stingrays usually swim away if approached. They rarely attack people. On September 4, 2006, however, a ray killed TV star Steve Irwin. While filming a nature movie, Irwin swam near Australia's Great Barrier Reef. Holding a camera, he swam over the top of a ray. Another camera operator filmed the ray from the front. In a second, the ray's tail flipped up. The poisonous tail pierced Irwin's chest. The ray was only acting naturally after being boxed in. Sadly, the world lost a popular TV star who taught people a lot about nature.

Sea snakes are found in the surface zone of the Indian and Pacific oceans. Some **species** are poisonous. Luckily, most are out of range of beaches and swimmers. Sea snakes have been known to form large groups in the ocean, sometimes in the millions.

The Portuguese man-of-war has an air bladder on top.

Chapter 3

In the Middle

Middle waters: From 660 to 3,300 feet (201 to 1,005 m)

The water gets darker the deeper you go. The creatures in the middle waters swim in a blue-black world. The fish are black or silver-gray, like swimming ghosts. Other creatures, such as shrimp and jellyfish, are bright shades of orange and purple.

Smooth anglerfish

The coelacanth sees well in dim light.

MEET THE COELACANTH

The strange-looking coelacanth (SEE-lah-kanth) lives in the middle zone. It is one of the oldest species of fish. Scientists used to think this fish had died out 65 million years ago. Then a fisherman caught one near South Africa in 1938. Scientists believe the species is related to fish that crawled ashore to become the first land animal. Coelacanths have fins that are like legs.

Coelacanths eat just about anything that fits in their mouths. The remains of animals and other matter that sink from the surface zone feed the animals of the middle zone.

BODIES IN BALANCE

The pressure at this depth is enough to crush an unprotected human. Why are the creatures of the middle zone not crushed? These creatures are "pressurized." The pressure inside their bodies is the same as the pressure outside.

Strange but True

In most animal species, the male is larger than the female. This is not true of deep-sea anglerfish in the middle waters. Females can grow to be 3 feet (1 m) long. Males are only about 1.5 inches (4 centimeters) long. The male attaches to the female. Her skin grows around him. Some of his body parts disappear, making him completely dependent on her.

SHINING A COLD LIGHT

It is a dark, cold world in the middle zone. But there are ghostly flashes of light. Many of the animals that live in this zone exhibit **bioluminescence**. That is light produced by a chemical reaction inside their bodies. Bioluminescence is a "cool" light that shines without making heat. Scientists are studying bioluminescent creatures. Doctors hope to find ways to add cold-light chemicals to parts of the human body. Using the light, doctors can better track cell growth, for example.

LIGHTS IN ACTION

Ocean animals use their "night lights" to their advantage. The lights help with hunting. The anglerfish living at this level have something that looks like a fishing pole at the front of the head. The fish stay still as the pole flashes to attract prey. Then the anglers snap their powerful jaws shut. The fish swallow their meals whole.

Light helps the hunted, too. Decapod shrimp vomit a cloud of blue light to blind their attackers. Lantern fish use lights on their bellies to hide from hunters. How? From below, the glowing fish are hard to see against the dim daylight coming from the ocean's surface.

A number of other animals use light as a kind of "burglar alarm." The light attracts larger animals. Then the larger animals can gobble up whatever is attacking the glowing creature.

Bioluminescent creatures of this zone glow in blue-green colors. Those colors of light transmit best through water.

The anglerfish has sharp teeth you can nearly see through.

Fishing for a Cure
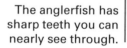

Osamu Shimomura won a Nobel Prize in chemistry in 2008. As a young man, he wondered why crystal jellyfish gave off green light. He collected more than 1 million of the jellyfish from waters around Washington state. He spent 40 years examining their glow. The scientist found a **protein** that makes blue light that is changed to green light by another protein, called GFP. GFP is very useful in medical research. For example, doctors can use GFP to find and track cancer cells in the human body.

These jellyfish appear green because of a special protein.

MOTORING TO MIDDLE WATERS

How do scientists know about creatures living in the middle waters and below? Humans cannot swim at those depths, even with special equipment. The pressure would crush a diver! To study marine life in those zones, oceanographers rely on machines.

A **remotely operated vehicle (ROV)** is an underwater robot. It is operated by a person at the surface. ROVs have mechanical arms to collect animals and samples of water and soil. The vehicles have lights, video cameras, and instruments to record images and take measurements.

A **submersible** is an underwater vehicle that can carry people to the ocean's depths. The U.S. submersible *Alvin* launched in 1964. It has carried thousands of scientists to the seafloor since then. The three-person sub has explored the sunken *Titanic* and carried out many other research missions.

ROVs go where divers cannot.

DIVING DEEP

U.S. engineers are building a new, more advanced submersible. The upgraded *Alvin* will dive deeper and move faster. It will stay down longer and carry more scientific gear.

A bar at the top will be used to hoist the vehicle.

ALVIN

Part of the old *Alvin*'s body is being reused.

New lights will brighten the inky-black ocean depths.

Five viewports will offer a good look at the undersea world.

Arms on either side of a "basket" will gather specimens.

21

Chapter 4

DOWN DEEP

Deep waters: From 3,300 to 13,000 feet (1,005 to 3,962 m)

Black, blacker, and *blackest* describe the next zone of the ocean. In deep waters, there is no sunlight at all. Night and day are alike. The creatures of this zone have been shaped by the darkness and crushing water pressure.

Viperfish

The glass squid is found only in the deep sea of the Southern Hemisphere.

In 2008, scientists found odd creatures in deep waters off Antarctica. Researchers found sea spiders the size of dinner plates, along with huge worms. Scientists say that large sizes are common in the Antarctic waters. They do not yet know why.

CREATURES OF THE DEEP

The creatures of the deep waters are unusual. The viperfish, for instance, has fangs so big that they cannot fit inside its mouth! The fangs curve back close to the creature's eyes. Scientists think these scary-looking fish swim at prey at high speed. The fish can stab the prey with their fangs.

THE EYES HAVE IT

Toward the top of this zone, the fish have very large eyes. The big eyes pick up the smallest amount of light. At 6,600 feet (2,011 m), however, the eyes of the fish become smaller. At the bottom of the zone, most fish have tiny eyes—or none at all! At that depth, there is no light.

Take a Look

A fish's eye is a lot like a person's eye. There are two big differences, though. The **lens** in a human eye can bend to focus light. The lens in a fish's eye cannot change shape. It can only move in and out to focus.

Because people's eyes are close together, we have **binocular vision**. Each eye sees a sightly different image. Then the brain combines the two images into one. Most fish have sideways-facing eyes. Each eye sees an image of a different area—on opposite sides of the fish's body. Fish have **monocular vision**.

23

STAYIN' ALIVE

At the top of the deep-water zone, the pressure is strong enough to crush concrete. At the bottom of the zone, the pressure is even stronger. So creatures that live in deep waters have some special **adaptations**.

Deep-sea animals have large heads that are not crushed by the water's weight. Their bodies and skeletons bend, so they can withstand the pressure. These creatures have a weak **nervous system**, so they do not feel pain as people do. These creatures tend to have long jaws and sharp teeth. Those adaptations help them hunt their prey.

The sperm whale has the largest brain of any living creature on Earth!

ECHOLOCATION

Extraordinary animals, such as the sperm whale, are able to move between this zone and the surface. Sperm whales use **echolocation** to find things in the dark. A sperm whale sends out sounds that bounce off objects and return to the whale. The greater the distance, the longer the sound takes to return. Sperm whales also have a special organ in the head. This organ allows them to withstand the pressure of the depths without damage.

The Deep-Sea Chain of Life

A **food chain** is a system of animals and plants that depend on one another for food. The deep-sea food chain, like most food chains on Earth, depends on the Sun. Plankton take in energy from the Sun on the surface. The plankton are eaten by other creatures. Another set of creatures eats the plankton eaters.

The surface waters are like a "soup" that drips down to the depths. Bits of biological matter, from **viruses** and **bacteria** to pieces of dead whales, rain down to the bottom. Along the way, creatures gobble up many of the bits. Those creatures, in turn, become meals for predators. Without the sunlight and plants at the top, however, the chain would be broken.

What's for Dinner?

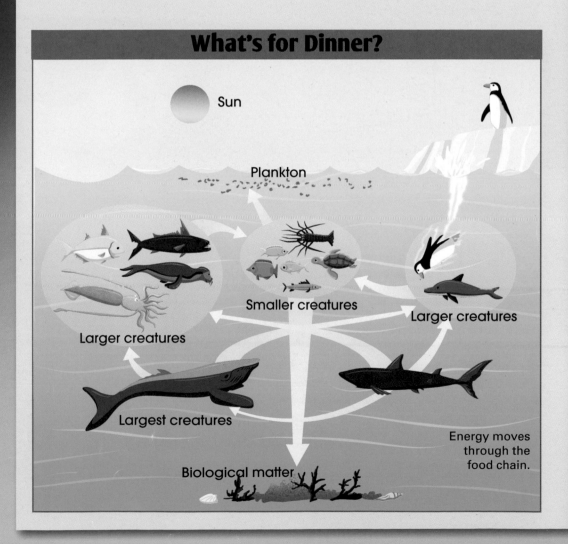

Sun

Plankton

Smaller creatures

Larger creatures

Larger creatures

Largest creatures

Biological matter

Energy moves through the food chain.

DEEP-SEA VAMPIRE

The deep waters hold some truly unusual creatures. One of the strangest is the vampire squid. This animal looks as if it belongs on another planet! Though called a vampire, the squid does not drink blood. Its name comes from the fang-like spikes on its legs.

The large fins at the top of its body look like big ears. This creature has the largest eyes of any animal in relation to its body size. The vampire squid has a soft body only about 6 inches (15 cm) long. Yet its eyes are the size of a large dog's eyes. This squid is covered with spots that produce light. The vampire squid can turn itself on and off like a lightbulb!

A "cape" of webbed skin connects the vampire squid's eight arms.

SQUID OR OCTOPUS?

How are squid and octopuses alike? Both creatures have arms attached directly to their heads. Both animals have hard beaks to break food. How can you tell them apart? Octopuses have eight arms. Squid have eight arms and two long tentacles. Most squid have fins. Octopuses have no fins. Octopuses are completely soft. Squid have a stiff structure, known as a pen, which is like a bending backbone. Octopuses live in dens on the seafloor. There, the females tend their eggs, and the octopuses hide from predators. Squid live in the open ocean.

Octopuses use their eight arms to swim and to crawl along the ocean floor.

FAST FACT
Thanks to special cells in their skin, octopuses can change color. They can blend into the background or show off with flashes of bright color.

The deep-sea dragonfish uses a glowing light to attract prey.

FAST FACT
The dragonfish seems to like to brag! It sometimes uses its lights to signal that it has found a mate.

The dragonfish has sidelights.

DRAGONS OF THE DEEP

The deep-sea dragonfish is small in size. Yet this creature is forceful! It is one of the more unforgettable creatures of the deep. The deep-sea dragonfish has a large head. Its mouth is filled with sharp teeth. The dragonfish has a long **barbel** attached to its chin. The barbel is a thin feeler, like a whisker. At the end of the barbel is a bioluminescent part called a **photophore**.

The dragonfish uses its photophore as a fishing lure. The lure flashes off and on and waves back and forth. The light attracts other creatures, which swim closer. Then the dragonfish snaps up the approaching fish in its powerful jaws.

The dragonfish also has photophores along its sides. Scientists think the fish uses these lights to attract other dragonfish. The sidelights may also confuse larger creatures that might attack the dragonfish from below.

28

THE FANGTOOTH

The fangtooth is a fearsome deep-water fish. It gets its name from its huge teeth. The teeth are the largest teeth of any fish, relative to its size.

This creature has a short body and a large head. Its eyes are very small. Yet the fangtooth has a keen ability to sense movement in the water. Scientists believe that the fish goes to upper waters at night to feed. Then the fangtooth returns to the depths during the day.

The fangtooth's long bottom teeth fit into "pockets" in the mouth so that they don't pierce the fish's brain!

FAST FACT
The fangtooth is only a few inches long. Yet its longest teeth are about the size of a human's teeth!

Chapter 5

Deeper, Deepest

Deeper waters: From 13,000 to 20,000 feet (3,962 to 6,096 m)

Deepest waters: From 20,000 to 36,200 feet (6,096 to 11,034 m)

Deep-sea shrimp can survive extreme cold and heat.

The ocean cannot get any blacker below the deep waters. Yet it can get much colder! In the deeper and deepest zones, the temperature is just above freezing.

PLANT-FREE ZONE

The zone of deeper waters includes most of Earth's oceans, except for the underwater mountains and ridges. No plants grow at these depths. All the living things have two jobs: to eat other animals and to avoid being eaten. Every creature here is a **carnivore**, or meat eater.

Most of the creatures in this zone are either very small or very large. Few known creatures are in between. Deep-sea shrimp, for example, are big. They can be 12 inches (30 cm) long. These shrimp can have **antennae** twice that length.

Sea urchins live in this zone, too. These animals are enclosed in a round shell. The type of sea urchins found at these depths measure 12 inches (30 cm) around. That is 10 times the size of sea urchins that live in shallow water.

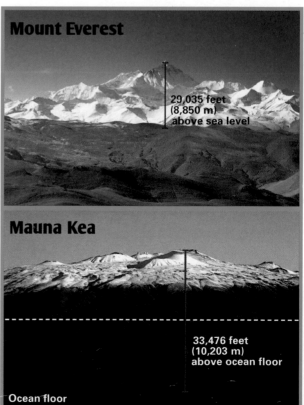

Sea urchins have hundreds of tiny tube feet that they use to move about.

Mount Everest

29,035 feet (8,850 m) above sea level

Mauna Kea

33,476 feet (10,203 m) above ocean floor

Ocean floor

FAST FACT
Mount Everest is the highest peak on land. Measured from its base on the ocean floor, Mauna Kea in Hawaii is the world's tallest mountain, however.

THE BOTTOM OF THE WORLD

The deepest part of the ocean is sometimes called the **hadal zone**. This zone begins where undersea plains drop off. The drop-offs are holes many miles or kilometers deep. These cracks reach to the very bottom of the world. The hadal zone includes **trenches**, or valleys, all around the Pacific Ocean. The coast of Central and South America and the northeast Indian Ocean also have many trenches. Deep canyons exist in the seafloor in the northeast Caribbean and the South Atlantic, too.

The hadal zone is completely dark and cold. At the bottom of the hadal zone, the pressure is impossible to imagine!

Sea anemones attach themselves to solid objects, such as rocks.

Nearly 1,300 kinds of sea cucumbers are known to exist.

The sabellid worm lives in tubes made of mud and slimy **mucus**.

IN THE TRENCHES

The trenches of the Pacific reach 36,200 feet (11,034 m) down. Few animals call the undersea valleys home. Some sea cucumbers, sea anemones, and worms populate this zone.

One creature at home here is a type of **amphipod**, an animal related to lobsters. Amphipods live all over the world. Yet it was still a surprise when scientists pulled a specimen from Challenger Deep in the Mariana Trench. Challenger Deep is the deepest known place in the ocean.

The deepest-dwelling fish is part of the **brotulid** family. Brotulids are nearly eyeless. These sightless fish live near the bottom of trenches. Brotulids have been found in the Puerto Rico Trench, living nearly 5 miles (8 km) down!

Who Was Hades?

Hadal means "like Hades." In Greek mythology, Hades was the god of the underworld. Gradually, his name also came to describe the place that he ruled. Hades was a gloomy, dark, and silent place— like the ocean depths.

THE GIANT SQUID

The largest known creatures in the deepest waters are squid. The giant squid is enormous. Males grow to a length of about 46 feet (14 m). Females are a bit shorter, at 43 feet (13 m). The giant squid has the biggest eye in the animal kingdom. One eye is about the size of a person's head!

FACTS GET CLEARER

Scientists are only now beginning to learn more about these mysterious creatures. Giant squid feed on deep-sea fish and on other species of squid. They catch prey using their two long tentacles. The squid's tentacles and eight arms have circular suction cups. The squid draws prey toward its strong beak. The beak, which is like a parrot beak, cuts into the victims. The beak shreds the prey so that the squid can swallow its food.

Giant squid have well-developed nervous systems and complicated brains. Scientists believe these animals are intelligent. The only known predator of the giant squid is the sperm whale. The sperm whale has been known to dive to great depths to catch giant squid.

FAST FACT

Scientists have found evidence of an even larger squid. The colossal squid's tentacles have sharp hooks for catching prey.

A squid can draw water into the main part of its body, called the **mantle**. Then the squid squirts out a jet of water to move fast.

PARTS OF A SQUID

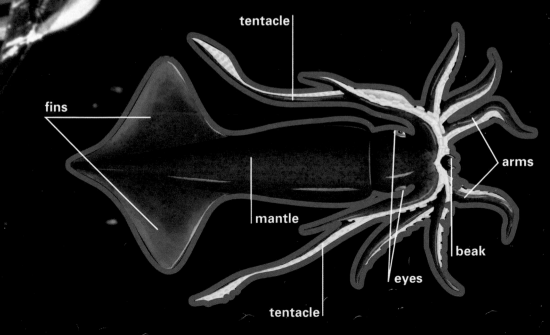

tentacle

fins

arms

mantle

beak

eyes

tentacle

Chapter 6

Gardens of the Dark Sea

One of the greatest ocean discoveries happened almost by accident. In 1977, researchers were studying breaks in the seafloor. While searching near the Galápagos Islands in the Pacific Ocean, the scientists found underwater vents. The vents are surrounded by unusual life-forms.

U.S. scientists were aboard the *Alvin* submarine when they discovered **hydrothermal vents**. These hot spots are cracks in Earth's crust. From the cracks, hot water rises into the cold water of the seafloor. The fluid is filled with minerals. Nearby, strange animals live in what look like undersea gardens.

Clams, mussels, and tube worms live near the vents. Many of the clams are more than 1 foot (0.3 m) long. Snakelike tube worms wave like long grass in the currents. The tube worms are up to 3.5 feet (1 m) long.

Shrimp live among the mussels at a hydrothermal vent.

SECRETS OF THE VENTS

The vents continue to give up their secrets. In 2008, the hottest water on Earth was found in a vent. Scientists say the water was so hot, it was something between a liquid and a gas. Water leaving the vents can be 752 degrees Fahrenheit (400 degrees Celsius). Other scientists discovered that viruses and bacteria around the vents mix in ways that are unusual. The viruses split the bacteria. The process produces a new kind of material. That discovery could be important in medical and other scientific research.

FAST FACT

The bacteria in undersea vents can live in hotter temperatures than any other creature on Earth can.

Tube worms and mussels make their home at a hydrothermal vent in the Pacific Ocean.

POISONOUS WATERS

Unlike other creatures in the deepest ocean, the animals at the vents grow fast. The creatures enjoy an energy source in the hot water escaping the vent. This seems strange at first. The vent water is poisonous, after all. It is filled with hydrogen sulfide, a gas that kills most living things.

Here is a life system that does not depend on the Sun for warmth. The animals at the vents live on bacteria that they filter from the water. They also eat films of bacteria off the rocks.

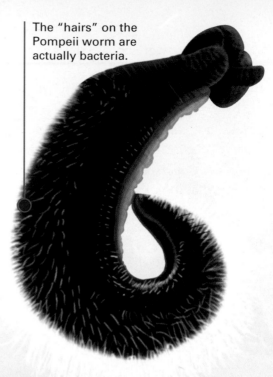

The "hairs" on the Pompeii worm are actually bacteria.

WEIRD AND WONDERFUL

Many new animal communities have been found in the world's oceans. Among the recent discoveries is a snail covered with iron scales. Another is the Pompeii worm, which lives happily in temperatures of 176 degrees F (80 degrees C). The worms, which are 4 inches (10 cm) long, live inside papery tubes attached to the vents.

The yeti crab was found deep in the water off the coast of Chile, in South America. The blind creature traps bacteria in the bristly hairs on its legs. The crab is named for the yeti, the hairy snowman of legends.

The yeti crab is a cousin of the better-known hermit crab.

YOU DO IT!

How a Hydrothermal Vent Works

What You Need
- large glass container
- small bottle
- food coloring
- 12-inch (30-cm) length of string
- hot and cold water

What You Do
Step 1
Fill a large container with very cold water.

Step 2
Tie a string around the mouth of a small bottle.

Step 3
Fill the bottle with hot water. Add a few drops of food coloring.

Step 4
Lower the bottle into the large container. Try not to spill the colored water!

WHAT DO YOU THINK?

Scientists have found colonies of sea life that do not need oxygen. What might this discovery mean about the possibility of life on other planets?

What Happened?
The colored water rises, just as hot water rises from the vents.

Chapter 7

Danger Above and Below

The deep ocean is far removed from human activity. Yet even the hidden sea is under attack by humans. Rising temperatures, harmful fishing practices, and pollution are affecting underwater life.

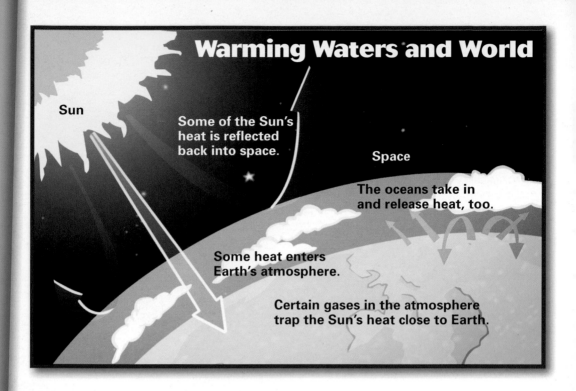

Warming Waters and World

Sun

Some of the Sun's heat is reflected back into space.

Space

The oceans take in and release heat, too.

Some heat enters Earth's atmosphere.

Certain gases in the atmosphere trap the Sun's heat close to Earth.

A WARMING WORLD

Global warming is the overall rise in average temperatures on Earth. The warming is caused, in part, by the burning of **fossil fuels**, which releases certain gases into the air. Those gases act like a greenhouse, trapping the Sun's warmth close to Earth.

Ocean temperatures rise as the **atmosphere** warms. The number of **phytoplankton** drops in warmer water. Phytoplankton are tiny plants that form the basis of the ocean food chain.

Carbon dioxide and other gases also cause an increase of **acid** in seawater. The acid is harmful to some ocean creatures. Higher amounts of acid are threatening the marine food chain.

GOING, GOING, GONE FISHIN'

Scientists are also worried that a number of deep-sea fish are close to dying out because of fishing methods. Many fishing crews drag huge nets across the bottom of the ocean. The result is sometimes the destruction of whole **habitats** and the creatures in them.

Deep-sea fish produce fewer offspring than most fish do. The deep dwellers also grow more slowly than fish in shallow or surface waters. It is not easy for deep-sea fish to replace the fish destroyed by bottom fishing.

41

Close to Home

According to a recent fish count, the deep-sea fish most endangered by fishing in the North Atlantic are as follows:

- roundhouse grenadier
- spiny eel
- blue hake
- onion-eye grenadier
- spinytail skate

Many deep-sea fish, including the grenadier, are dying out.

GRENADIERS IN DANGER

In the North Atlantic, some fish are disappearing. The roundhouse grenadier and the onion-eye grenadier are very rare. Officials say the fish may disappear forever.

Scientists worry about the destruction of the deep-sea **ecosystem**. "Here are fishes that nobody has heard of, that nobody really cares about, but we take as part of the fact that the whole ecosystem is being [hurt]," marine biologist Richard Haedrich told redOrbit News.

There are many things you can do to help protect ocean life. For instance, you can join an organized beach cleanup.

Kids Can Help

You do not need a submersible or a degree in oceanography to help protect endangered sea life. Here are some things you can do to make a difference.

- Eat only some kinds of seafood. Much seafood today is grown on farms along both U.S. coasts. Have your parents check whether the seafood they buy is "farm raised." Also, ask your parents whether their favorite restaurant serves seafood that is not endangered.

- Eat organic, locally grown food. Organic food is raised with fewer or no chemicals. The runoff of chemicals from farms is a major polluter of the oceans. The chemicals run from land to sea, harming ocean habitats.

- Use phosphate-free soap. Phosphates are chemicals in soaps and some detergents. The chemicals enter the runoffs from cities and towns. The chemicals encourage growth of ocean organisms called **algae**. The algae can choke out other sea life.

- Do not put poison, such as car oil, down your drain. Poisons run from homes into rivers and eventually into the sea. Poisons can harm water creatures.

- Support ocean **conservation** organizations. Find a committed organization, such as ORCA (Ocean Research and Conservation Association). Many groups work to protect the sea. Learn about the serious problems threatening ocean life.

43

SCIENCE AT WORK

MARINE BIOLOGIST

Job: Marine biologists study the living organisms of the sea, from the simplest plants to the largest whales and their relationship to their environment.

Job Outlook: Employment is expected to grow 9 percent by 2016.

Earnings: $25,000 to $35,000 to start, up to $150,000 or more for supervisors, with a median income of $76,320 (2006)

Source: Bureau of Labor Statistics

Conversation With a Marine Biologist

Shirley Pomponi is executive director and research professor at the Harbor Branch Oceanographic Institute, in Fort Pierce, Florida.

WHEN YOU WERE YOUNGER, WHAT SPARKED YOUR INTEREST IN THE MARINE WORLD?

Family vacations to the New Jersey shore were (and still are) a highlight. But when I was in college, I had the opportunity to take a summer course in marine ecology in St. Croix, Virgin Islands, and that's what really led me to choose my career path.

HOW DOES YOUR WORK BENEFIT THE PUBLIC?

Our drug discovery work may someday soon lead to a cure for cancer. Our research on sea grasses, **coral reefs**, and marine mammals will contribute to a healthier coastal ocean—which has a direct impact on our own health and well-being. Our aquaculture research is developing techniques to grow seafood, so we don't have to harvest fish and shellfish from the wild. Those are just a few of the benefits.

TELL US MORE ABOUT YOUR SPECIFIC AREA OF RESEARCH.

I work on sponges that produce chemicals that may be useful as drugs to treat diseases, like cancer. ... I'm trying to grow the sponge cells and get them to produce the chemicals in the lab.

WHAT IS THE WEIRDEST CREATURE YOU HAVE ENCOUNTERED?

I guess the one that sticks out the most is probably one of the first weird deep-sea creatures I encountered: a purple sea cucumber that doesn't crawl around on the bottom but swims gracefully in very deep water, just above the bottom.

FIND OUT MORE

● BOOKS

Head, Honor. *Amazing Fish* (Amazing Life Cycles). Pleasantville, NY: Gareth Stevens Publishing, 2008.

Hodge, Susie. *Ocean Survival* (Extreme Habitats). Pleasantville, NY: Gareth Stevens Publishing, 2008.

Schatz, Dennis. *Totally Sea Creatures*. Berkeley: Silver Dolphin Books, 2004.

Woodward, John. *Midnight Zone* (Exploring the Oceans). Chicago: Heinemann, 2004.

● WEB SITES

Dive and Discover
www.divediscover.whoi.edu
This site, part of the Woods Hole Oceanographic Institution, takes you on a virtual expedition to the ocean floor.

Ocean Explorer
www.oceanexplorer.noaa.gov
This National Oceanic and Atmospheric Administration (NOAA) site offers fun ways to explore the undersea world.

Sea and Sky
www.seasky.org/deep-sea/deep-sea-intro.html
Sea and Sky offers sound effects and more from the strange animals in the sea.

Publisher's note to educators and parents: Our editors have carefully reviewed these web sites to ensure that they are suitable for children. Many web sites change frequently, however, and we cannot guarantee that a site's future contents will continue to meet our high standards of quality and educational value. Be advised that children should be closely supervised whenever they access the Internet.

GLOSSARY

acid: a chemical substance that can harm the environment when present in rain, snow, or seawater

adaptations: changes in form or function that help an organism better survive

algae: simple plantlike organisms that lack roots, stems, and leaves yet can make food by using the energy of sunlight

amphipod: a kind of sea or freshwater animal that is related to lobsters

antennae: a pair of sense organs on the head of certain animals

atmosphere: (1) a layer of air around Earth; (2) a unit of measure for pressure

bacteria: one-celled living things

barbel: a thin feeler, resembling a whisker, on the lips or jaws of some fish

binocular vision: the ability to focus with two eyes

bioluminescence: the chemical generation of light by some organisms

brotulid: a deep-water fish that is nearly eyeless

carnivore: an animal that mainly eats meat

climate: average weather conditions over time

conservation: protection and management of natural resources

coral reefs: ridges near the ocean surface that are made up of the skeletons of tiny sea animals called corals

currents: steady onward movements, especially of a fluid such as water

echolocation: a means of locating an object based on emission and reflection of sound

ecosystem: all the living and nonliving things in a certain area

food chain: a community of organisms that eat one another

fossil fuels: fuels formed from plants and animals that died millions of years ago

global warming: the overall warming of Earth's surface over time

habitats: natural environments in which plants or animals live

hadal zone: the area of the ocean with deep trenches

hydrothermal vents: cracks in the ocean floor produced by the action of extremely hot water in Earth's crust

lens: a structure in animal eyes that focuses light

mantle: the main body part of certain animals, such as squid and octopuses

marine biology: the study of plants and animals of the ocean

monocular vision: the ability of each eye to work separately

mucus: a thick fluid that protects certain body tissues

nervous system: the body system that uses information from the senses to control other body systems

oceanography: the study of the oceans

photophore: a light organ on many deep-sea fish

phytoplankton: plant matter in plankton

plankton: tiny plants and simple animals eaten by fish and other water animals

predators: animals that hunt, kill, and eat other animals

prey: an animal that is hunted for food by a predator

protein: a substance that is fundamental to living cells

remotely operated vehicle (ROV): a robotic vehicle controlled by an operator outside the machine

satellites: objects that go around something else, such as the Moon around Earth

sea level: the level of the sea between high and low tide, used in measurements

species: kinds or classes of organisms

submersible: a small submarine used for deep ocean research

tentacles: long, thin growths around the head or mouth of certain animals without backbones

trenches: valleys on the ocean floor

viruses: tiny living things that cannot grow outside a host

Hammerhead shark

INDEX

About the Author

Charles Piddock is a former editor in chief at Weekly Reader Publishing. He has written and edited hundreds of articles for young people on world and national affairs, science, literature, and other topics. He has also been a Peace Corps volunteer in rural West Bengal, India.